Torii Haiku

ALSO BY DAVID H. ROSEN

Henry's Tower

Transforming Depression: Healing the Soul through Creativity

The Tao of Jung: The Way of Integrity

The Tao of Elvis

The Healing Spirit of Haiku (With Joel Weishaus)

Clouds and More Clouds

Lost in the Long White Cloud: Finding My Way Home

Time, Love and Licorice: A Healing Coloring Storybook

Spelunking through Life: A Collection of Haiku

Living with Evergreens: A Collection of Haiku

Patient-Centered Medicine: A Human Experience (With Uyen Hoang)

In Search of the Hidden Pond

The Alchemy of Cooking: Recipes with a Jungian Twist

White Rose, Red Rose: A Collection of Haiku (With Johnny Baranski)

Samantha the Sleuth & Zack's Hard Lesson

Torii Haiku

Profane to a Sacred Life

by
DAVID H. ROSEN

Foreword by Johnny Baranski

RESOURCE *Publications* • Eugene, Oregon

TORII HAIKU
Profane to a Sacred Life

Resource Publications
An Imprint of Wipf and Stock Publishers
199 W. 8th Ave., Suite 3
Eugene, OR 97401

www.wipfandstock.com

PAPERBACK ISBN: 978-1-5326-5709-2

Manufactured in the U.S.A.   05/15/18

For my wife, Lanara, a dear soul.

Haiku is humanized Nature.

- R.H. BLYTH[1]

Be not afraid of life.
Believe that life *is* worth living,
and your belief will help create the fact.

- WILLIAM JAMES[2]

1. Blyth, R.H. *A History of Haiku, Vol.1*. Tokyo: Hokuseido Press, 1963, p.28.

2. James, W. (1897). "Is Life Worth Living?" in *The WIll to Believe and Other Essays in Popular Philosophy*. New York: Dover.

Foreword

Gates. There are gates to keep us out and gates to keep us in. Garden gates, prison gates, gates to sacred places. There are healing gates like the Fountain Gate in old Jerusalem near the pool of Siloam whose waters cured the blind man in John's Gospel (7:9). Come walk with me now through a gate to healing moments, the sacred moments that are David Rosen's haiku.

Torii gate
fireflies show
the way

Johnny Baranski
August 2017

Prelude

With haiku we walk through a Torii gate from the profane to the sacred. As outlined in a previous volume, haiku is healing.[3] Poetry as active imagination helps people move in the direction of wholeness.[4]

This book began in 1978 when I wrote my first haiku. I ventured to a precipice overlooking a lake in Ontario, Canada and wrote this:

> Dawn on a spring sea -
> then a glittering
> from a thousand jumping fish

All haiku are based on healing moments. Hence, this volume is also a poetic memoir. My life's journey proceeds with dramatic changes after long gestation periods. The poems were written in various countries: Greece, Japan, China, Brazil, Switzerland, France, Holland, and our own.

3. Rosen, D.H. and J. Weishaus. 2014. *The Healing Spirit of Haiku*. Eugene, OR: Wipf & Stock.

4. Rosen, D.H. and C. Goodman. Eds. 2016. *Darkness Holding Light (A Collection of Poems by the Eugene Friends of Jung)*. Eugene: Oregon Resource Publications.

Some of these poems were previously published in the following journals and books:

Modern Haiku, Frogpond, Psychological Perspectives, Haiku Society of America Members' Anthologies, The Heron's Nest, Simply Haiku, Kernels, and Clouds and More Clouds, The Healing Spirit of Haiku (with Joel Weishaus), Spelunking through Life, Living with Evergreens, In Search of the Hidden Pond, and White Rose, Red Rose (with Johnny Baranski).

A calling
daring to be -
gentle grace

Love too young
breaks,
burns

Alone -
me
and the sea

Happiness -
bright red hibiscus
opens

Sometimes I listen
at times I talk
but always I sing

Anastasia
cleans the room every day —
her gold teeth sparkle

Scent of viburnum . . . spring is in the air

In the pond, the sky!

Wild winter rose. . .beauty and hurt

Tomorrow, I will be a marigold

Slug. . .
mentor for moving
through the world

Gnat. . .
thanks for reminding me of
our short lives

Red dragonfly
came to visit -
alone, but not alone

Handicapped grey beard rounding the pond

Buddhism -
no ego or self
to kill

Flowers grow and
leaves fall -
Nature's way

The green hills of spring wash over me

Hello!
fly in winter —
where am I?

Here, there, everywhere
Charlottesville

Heather Heyer
holding a deep red blossom. . .
died for peace

Holding this tiny flower
I, too
feel disconnected

Limbs of the live oak
touch the grass
lazy September Sunday

On mother earth -
every breath
simple and easy

On mother earth -
universal tree
upside down roots

On mother earth -
each spring
pure and flowing

On mother earth -
giant oaks and
their shadows

On mother earth -
ever present sun's rays and
moonbeams

On mother earth -
a puppy
wants to play

On mother earth -
verdant ferns
along the path

On mother earth -
after rain
sunbeam appears

On mother earth -
deep cave
black with light

On mother earth -
every step
gentle and measured

Watching solar eclipse
feeling inner eclipse

Light on the oaks
their deep green
shines

Lilacs blossom
birds fly north -
dream of a mountain to climb

Buddha nature
of a dog, a human
in full bloom

Mourning doves
chatter
at dusk

Old oaks
bend
toward the sun

Willow roams around
with her nose
on the ground

Hawk holds
ground squirrel -
despite the cries

Wind in the trees. . .
sounds like
water

- For Aidan

Frog pond
in front of our home. . .
comforting sounds

Clouds
and more clouds
lone black bird

Red cardinal atop
leafless ginkgo —
year of emptiness

Leaving academia -
joining my friends:
birds, trees, and wind

.

Village of thatched roofs
on a lush mountain
the monk's meal of greens

Sitting in the rain
waiting for the train
to nowhere

All this rain
from on-high. . .
another sigh

Walking in the rain
feeling the pain

Freezing rain. . .breaking heart

After the storm
greener greens -
dogwood buds open

Shadow burnt into wall -
rain falls, leaving no sound
behind

Leonard Cohen's
Hallelujah
on my mind

Everything I've done
& been. . .
my life

Many birds. . .one soul
  - by Lanara

Wanderer. . .in search of my soul

At the post office
waiting for the mail. . .
and my female

With my wife, everyday is Happy Valentine's Day

Married to a green goddess -
I keep growing

Belated honeymoon -
the rest of my life

As part of Nature -
every person
deserves a chance

Pond full -
yellowjacket
stings

Streetwalker
tells her story -
Eiffel Tower pales

Trees and windmills
emerge from water -
sailing in Holland

Torn asunder. . .putting back the pieces

At birth I died and was reborn

Mother dying. . .
full moon over
Kansas City, the world

Another year. . .where did the last one go?

Open door to dark room
watching the clock -
feeling uprooted

Living in paradise at the end of Camas Lane

In the parking lot
he held the Mumms
like a baby

Flowering tree
showered with mist -
smile on my face

Empty new home -
smell of redwoods
sound of a river

Peonies under
shade of yellow roses -
no one home

Falling leaves -
content to jump
and jitterbug

Glorious pink clouds
at sunset -
another one gone

Beads of
dewy friendship,
flowing forever

Numb -
arching vulture soars

Our lovely rescue dog, Willow, died.
But, his memory lives on.

Sitting in the sun,
a tear runs down my cheek -
Willow's gone

Splendor of a golden moon -
Willow crosses over

Flowering kale for an empty heart

Precious apple
fell near the tree. . .
bless Willow

Walking alone
with my friend
white butterfly

Slug trail on the porch . . .
now, I understand my life

MADLY SOBERING

I'd fallen, so I was referred to a specialist. Having had a similar dream image that same morning, I asked my neurologist, Dr. Joan Jensen, "What are all those white spots in the MRI of my brain?" In her direct, yet kind way, she said, "Those are scars." "Scars?" She responded, "Yes, sclerosis means scar." I nearly fell off the chair. Then she added, "MS is not a death sentence." That was eight years ago and I started taking medication and drastically changed my diet and life style. I recall the accurate and shocking response of my New Zealand poet friend, Ralph Woodward, "Madly Sobering." Comforting were the wise words of James Hillman, "A scar is the mark of soul in flesh." Hence, it's contact with the ancestors: Multiple Souls.

Light
in the darkness
the black sun

Under the Torii, we got married

ABOUT THE AUTHOR

David is the author and co-author of many books. They range from children's books to medical works, a memoir, as well as a coloring book and a cookbook. He is currently working on a second memoir. David also enjoys performing standup comedy under the name Dr. Nada. He lives in Eugene, Oregon, with his wife Lanara and their rescue dog Willow.

www.ingramcontent.com/pod-product-compliance
Lightning Source LLC
Chambersburg PA
CBHW071910110426
R18126600001B/R181266PG42743CBX00011B/3